THE
WISDEN
BOOK OF
CRICKET HE

BOWLERS

THE

WISDEN

BOOK OF

CRICKET HEROES

BOWLERS

ALAN LEE

Stanley Paul

London Sydney Auckland Johannesburg

Stanley Paul & Co. Ltd

An imprint of Century Hutchinson Ltd

62–65 Chandos Place, London WC2N 4NW

Century Hutchinson Australia (Pty) Ltd
89–91 Albion Street, Surry Hills, NSW 2010

Century Hutchinson New Zealand Limited
PO Box 40–086, Glenfield, Auckland 10

Century Hutchinson South Africa (Pty) Ltd
PO Box 337, Bergvlei 2012, South Africa

First published 1989
Reprinted 1989 (twice)
© Alan Lee 1989

Set in 11/13pt Plantin by Input Typesetting Ltd., London

Printed & Bound in Great Britain by Mackays of Chatham PLC, Letchworth.

British Library Cataloguing in Publication Data
Lee, Alan, 1954–
    The Wisden book of cricket heroes. Bowlers
    1. Cricket. Biographies. Collections
    I. Title
    796.35′8′0922
ISBN 0 09 173840 7

CONTENTS

Acknowledgement

The author and publishers would like to thank Adrian Murrell of All-Sport UK Ltd, who supplied all the photographs.

Introduction

Every cricket follower, no matter his age, fancies himself as a selector. Some may be more dogmatic than others, some more realistic, but I doubt if there is a single fan of our summer game who has not, at some time, indulged himself in picking an England team to beat the choice of the selectors, or a world team to beat the West Indies.

The great attraction is that the possibilities are endless and the responsibility nil. No-one is ever going to disprove your argument that a certain batting order is very much better than the one being persevered with by the official selectors; no-one is going to pit your World XI against Mars and show they are eminently beatable. Picking teams creates a theatre for healthy debate.

As a boy, I was forever frittering away time which ought to have been spent on school homework in the idle pursuit of choosing my own favourite England side, or a World side of left-handers, etc. I am lucky. The job I have now entitles me to go on record with my version of an England team before every Test Match. If the selectors' choices differ, I can criticize – but it is still their team which has to go out and be judged.

I jumped at the chance to select my own batting and bowling heroes for these two Wisden books. Wouldn't anyone? But when I actually sat down to condense the candidates to twenty, for each category, I began to experience the problems of the real selector. There were so many options, so many difficult decisions.

No doubt my choices will not meet with universal approval. I have omitted players reluctantly, included others tentatively. My only provisos were that everyone involved should have played Test cricket (in the case of Graeme Pollock, unofficial Tests) during the 1980s.

Now that I have made my choices and, in the pages which follow, sought to justify them, I have only one regret. I wish I could form some of these players into my own, Sunday afternoon team . . . now, that is a fantasy world.

TERRY ALDERMAN

RECORD 📖

Terence Michael Alderman was born in Perth, Western Australia on 12 June 1956. A right-arm fast-medium bowler of above-average height, he took five wickets on his debut for Western Australia in 1974–5, but had to wait another seven years before being picked for Australia. His Test debut was even more sensational – he took nine wickets – and in the six-match series he collected 42 victims, an Australian record against England. He made three further tours, and played a total of 22 Tests before joining the banned trip to South Africa in 1986 and suffering suspension. His Test career had already been interrupted by serious damage to his right shoulder, sustained when rugby-tackling a spectator who invaded the Perth ground during the 1982 Test with England.

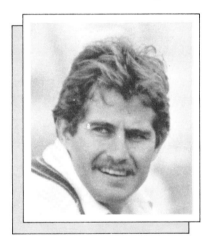

‘Alderman's selection for the tour had caused some surprise ’

— *Wisden*, on the 1981 series in which Alderman took 42 wickets

TECHNIQUE 🏏

A high level of skill, allied to apparently bottomless stamina are the hallmarks of Alderman's bowling. Not being a genuinely fast bowler, he has invariably found himself with the 'uphill and into the wind' role of the underrated dogsbody. In his case, however, the job is no insult. He frequently shared the bowling attack with the great Dennis Lillee, for Western Australia and at Test level, and he is swift to point out how helpful that was.

Lillee, indeed, was responsible for adding a vital edge to Alderman's bowling. He had, until 1981, been known as predominantly a swing bowler of only a little above medium pace, whose run-up was a gentle canter and whose delivery was a shade chest-on. Lillee suggested that he would be more successful in English conditions if he increased his pace and hit the seam. The results bear repetition – 42 wickets in the series – figures which delighted and astonished even his most fervent supporters. In two seasons with Kent, and another with Gloucestershire, Alderman has continued to show his aptitude for English pitches, so many of which encourage seam bowlers. He can move the ball in either direction off the pitch and continues to swing it sufficiently to make the batsman's life unpleasant.

HIGHLIGHTS 🏆

Terry Alderman might easily have chosen a different path to sporting fame. His father was an Australian Rules footballer who represented the state at half-back. Terry, one of five children, looked like following in his footsteps and, at school in Perth he took easily to football. His athletic father, however, had also been good enough at cricket to play for Western Australia at colts level, and it was this game which finally claimed the attentions of his son. In 1981, Australia had very good reason to be thankful.

They came to England with an odd mix of a team. The Chappell brothers had retired and although Lillee and Marsh remained, both were in the twilight of their playing days. Kim Hughes was captain and new names were emerging like Border, Lawson . . . and Alderman. The teacher from Perth, married to a girl from Derbyshire, found himself making his long-awaited Test debut just down the road at Nottingham. He did not waste the chance.

It was a low-scoring game, on a pitch well suited to seam bowling. Alderman, bowling long spells, counted Boycott and Botham among his four wickets as England were bowled out for 185, but this was still enough for a slender lead of six as the England seamers relished their turn. Now Lillee and Alderman really set to work. Alderman, never one to shirk hard work, bowled unchanged through the England second innings to take five for 62, completing match figures of nine for 130 on his debut. Even in such difficult conditions, a winning target of 132 was well within Australia's grasp and they got home by four wickets.

Their joy was short-lived. After a dull draw at Lord's, England scored three successive victories in Tests which will live forever in the folklore of the game. One man, however, came through the trauma with reputation enhanced, for in the course of those three games Alderman took another 26 wickets.

Ian Botham

Record 📖

Ian Terence Botham was born at Heswall, Cheshire on 24 November 1955. A right-arm bowler, medium to fast-medium pace, he spent two years on the MCC groundstaff at Lord's before joining Somerset in 1974. He played 13 seasons for the county, two as captain, but moved on to Worcestershire in 1987. Botham made his England debut against Australia in 1977 and took five wickets on his first Test day. He has now played 94 Tests, including 12 as captain, and his 373 wickets was, until recently, a world record. He has taken five or more wickets in a Test innings on 27 occasions, his best analysis being eight for 34 against Pakistan at Lord's in 1978. A serious back injury sidelined him for most of the 1988 season.

❝ In his prime, and when roused, he could bowl as fast as anyone in England ❞

Technique 🌀

When at his bowling peak, between 1978 and 1982, Ian Botham was an exuberant assassin of the very best batting in the world. Never content with bowling to contain and frustrate, Botham expressed his natural spirit of adventure through his remarkable range and, as is often the case with one who experiments so freely, his wickets frequently accrued from the worst ball in an over.

His greatest asset was to bowl the awayswinger at will. He would swing the ball late and abruptly, making him almost unplayable when conditions were right. Several times, on a humid, overcast morning in Test cricket, Botham would apparently have opposition batsmen on a piece of string, teasing them before finishing them off, his right fist raised and that familiar grin huge as he rushed down the pitch for congratulations.

He has a very correct, sideways-on bowling action (many people make the mistake of believing that Botham gets by on eye and flair, whereas his technique with bat and ball is immaculate). In his prime, and when roused, he could also bowl as fast as anyone in England and his liberal use of the bouncer earned him a share of wickets and a share of rebukes.

HIGHLIGHTS

Just two weeks after his staggering century had transformed the Headingley Test Match of 1981, Botham was at it again. This time, his heroics were with the ball but, although much briefer than in Leeds, they were every bit as devastating. The Australians, apparently well set for a victory to restore pride and composure, and put them ahead again in the series, were once more beaten by a whisker amid national hysteria. Botham was their tormentor again.

This time, there had seemed no way out for England. The big Sunday crowd at Edgbaston knew in their hearts that miracles could not be repeated. Australia had outplayed England for three days and now, even on a wearing pitch which was taking appreciable turn, their task of scoring 142 with nine wickets intact seemed simple enough. Anyway, the spectators told each other with resigned amusement, Botham did not bowl spin, did he?

The first indications of drama in store came during the morning session as Bob Willis, who shared the Headingley headlines, bowled another superb spell, dismissing Dyson and Hughes, the Australian captain. At 29 for three Australia were wobbling but Border and Yallop, two eminently skilful left-handers, refused to panic. They put on 58, slowly but surely. At 87 for three, with only 64 wanted, the game looked safe.

John Emburey made the breakthrough – helped of course, by Botham, who caught Yallop at silly mid-off. Border remained until the total had crept up to 105 and Mike Brearley then asked Botham to bowl. At first he was reluctant, reasoning that Willey, the second spinner, would be more effective. But when Emburey dismissed Border with an unplayable ball, it was a different story. Botham roared in, cheered every step by the crowd, and in 28 deliveries he took the last five Australian wickets for just one run. England won by 29 runs. Australians could scarcely believe it. Neither could many in the crowd. But this was a wonderful cricketer in a purple patch, a time when he could do no wrong. He gave the whole country a lift during that glorious summer of '81.

SYLVESTER CLARKE

RECORD 📖

Sylvester Theophilus Clarke was born at Christ Church, Barbados on 11 December 1954. A right-arm fast bowler, he made his debut for Barbados in 1977–8 and first played county cricket for Surrey in 1979, winning his cap the following year. The intense competition among West Indian fast bowlers restricted him to 11 Test appearances between 1977 and 1982 but he was probably on the brink of a regular place when his decision to join the unsanctioned tour of South Africa earned him a life ban from the West Indies team. He has since played with great success for the South African Currie Cup champions, Transvaal. He took 42 wickets in Tests and also played ten limited-overs internationals.

' Clarke can be a frightening sight from the batsman's end as he pounds in to bowl '

TECHNIQUE 《

At 6 feet 2 inches, and weighing 15 stones, Sylvester Clarke can be a frightening sight from the batsman's end as he pounds in to bowl. He does not take a particularly long run-up but is quickly into a sprint and, watching from a safe distance, it is possible to imagine the ground shaking as he approaches the crease.

He has been prone to injury during his career, which is not exactly surprising for such a big man, but when fully fit and motivated he is regarded by many batsmen as the quickest and most hostile of all the world's new-ball bowlers. His delivery is too chest-on to be thought strictly correct but his arm comes through extremely rapidly and batsmen say it is hard to pick up his length.

Clarke bowls a ferocious bouncer and a very effective yorker, usually slipped through a batsman's defences as he looks to get onto the back foot. Surrey have used him as their main strike bowler for the past decade and few county batsmen look forward to the experience!

HIGHLIGHTS 🏆

Throughout the 1950s, Surrey were the dominant force in English county cricket. They won the Championship no fewer than seven times and with a mighty batting line-up which included Micky Stewart and Peter May, plus bowlers of the calibre of Alec Bedser and Jim Laker, they were untouchable. Times have changed. The Championship pennant has flown at The Oval only once in the past 30 years and the most recent honour won by the club was the NatWest Trophy in 1982. Much of the credit for this lonely but welcome triumph went to Sylvester Clarke.

The final itself was an anti-climax to the usual capacity crowd at Lord's. Warwickshire, surprise finalists, were put into bat and found no answer to Surrey's six-strong seam attack. They were all out for only 158, Clarke taking two for 17 in 11.2 miserly overs, five of them maidens. Surrey knocked off the required runs for the loss of only one wicket. Later, once the celebrations had run their course, the players will doubtless have reflected that their real final was won the previous month, when the semi-final draw pitted them against their neighbours from across the Thames, Middlesex.

For Surrey, in particular, a great deal of London pride was at stake in this game. Under Mike Brearley, Middlesex had become the strongest side in England and they were on the way to winning the Championship for the fourth time in seven years. Surrey had become very much the poor neighbour and this was not a label which hung comfortably on those in office at The Oval. Clarke ensured that, for a day at least, Surrey ruled the capital.

Chasing a Surrey total of 205 in the statutory 60 overs, and no doubt confident of achieving it, Middlesex were wrecked by Clarke's first, six-over spell. Bowling intimidatingly fast, he took the wickets of Slack, Brearley, Tomlins and, crucially, Gatting for only six runs. There was no way back from the poverty of 17 for four and Clarke did not even need to return for a second spell. He did, however, finish the job by catching his fellow Barbadian Wayne Daniel as Middlesex were bowled out for a humiliating score of 80. Surrey supporters will tell you that Clarke earned his season's wages in that day alone.

Kapil Dev

Record 📖

Kapil Dev Nikhanj was born in the Punjab town of Chandigarh, northern India on 6 January 1959. A right-arm fast-medium bowler, also a hard-hitting middle-order batsman, he made his debut for Haryana when only 16 and took six for 39. He first played Test cricket in October 1978, against Pakistan at Faisalabad, and is now approaching 100 Tests for India. He holds the records for the youngest player ever to score 1,000 Test runs (21 years 27 days) and to take 100 Test wickets (two days fewer). He is also the only Indian to have taken more than 300 Test wickets. Kapil spent four years as captain of India and led them to triumph in the 1983 World Cup. He has played county cricket for Northamptonshire and Worcestershire.

‘ He was like a visitor from another planet when he appeared on the Indian scene ’

Technique ⚫

For many years, Indian cricket appealed to the romantics among cricket-watchers, those who liked the fine and delicate things in the game. They had plenty of wristy, elegant batsmen and an abundance of twirling, teasing spin bowlers. But there was not a fast bowler in sight worthy of the description.

Kapil Dev was like a visitor from another planet when he appeared on the Indian scene in such spectacular style, taking vast collections of wickets for his state, Haryana. He quickly made his mark in Test cricket, too, and in the past ten years he has been a model of consistency despite having to shoulder an enormous workload as the only genuine strike bowler in the Indian side.

His bowling has about it an impression of bounce and vibrancy. He may sometimes walk back to his mark slower than spectators would like but when he turns, head suddenly raised as if from prayer, he gallops lightly in to the crease, where a final leap is followed by a model delivery. His left arm is high, his body classically sideways on. Through such textbook perfection Kapil is able to swing the ball liberally, his outswinger causing particular problems over the years. At a sturdy 6 feet 3 inches he is also capable of deceptive pace off the pitch, often surprising batsmen with steep bounce.

HIGHLIGHTS 🏆

Whatever else he may achieve, and bear in mind he is only just past his 30th birthday, Kapil Dev will be remembered both as the youngest man to achieve the two great Test milestones (1,000 runs and 100 wickets) and the captain who led India to their logic-defying triumph in the 1983 Prudential World Cup. If this is quite right and proper, there is also another side to the career of possibly the most charismatic cricketer ever to come out of India.

He was neither bred to be a cricketer nor, for some while, did he seem destined to be a fast bowler. Indeed Kapil's first, hesitant progress in the game was made as a spin bowler and the facts that he was (a) remote from the game's centres, and (b) not exactly obsessed by it can be judged through his admission that the first Test Match he ever saw was the first one he played in.

He had, by then, made a short tour of East Africa. This was largely at the instigation of the great 'Sunny' Gavaskar who had been sufficiently impressed when Kapil bowled to him in a domestic match to recommend his selection. Gavaskar recalls how Kapil, still a raw teenager, was always keen to learn from his seniors. He also recalls how he improved so dramatically on that trip that he earned selection for the full Test tour to Pakistan later the same year.

Even then, he was not expected to force his way into the Test team and yet, through possessing a pace and vitality not seen in an Indian attack before, he could not be ignored. He was named for the opening Test at Faisalabad but, to his dismay, it was played on a perfect batting pitch.

Undaunted, Kapil extracted some unsuspected bounce from the surface. After only a few overs Sadiq Mohammed, the experienced Pakistan opener, decided discretion was the better part of valour and called for a helmet to replace his cap. Not a moment too soon . . . in the next over a bouncer from Kapil rattled against Sadiq's helmet and flew to the boundary for four byes. From that moment on, Kapil Dev was accepted as a member of the Test fraternity and respected as someone who could produce fire and fear where, for so many years, none had existed.

GRAHAM DILLEY

RECORD

Graham Roy Dilley was born in Dartford, Kent on 18 May 1959. A right-arm fast bowler, he played for Kent for ten seasons after his debut in 1977. In 1987 he joined Worcestershire and, a year later, helped them to the double of Championship and Sunday League. Dilley's England career began in the winter of 1979–80, when he toured Australia, but it was the mid-1980s before he held down a regular place. Often troubled by injuries, he missed the entire 1984 season after coming home early from a tour of Pakistan with a serious back injury. He made a full recovery to reclaim his England place and gain full acceptance as the premier strike bowler in the country. He is now well past 100 wickets after 39 Test Matches.

❝I'm resigned to the fact that I may end up in a wheelchair at any time❞

Graham Dilley

TECHNIQUE

That old saying about every cloud having a silver lining could easily be applied to Graham Dilley. In 1984 he might have been at his lowest ebb as injury threatened his entire future in cricket. Yet out of this depressing period came a renewed determination, a remodelled action and an altogether tougher, more resilient character.

Dilley had always been good enough to succeed at high level. That was evident from his earliest matches for England. What was in question was his moral and physical fibre, his ability to overcome stresses and strains, and his fighting qualities when the chips were down. He did not play any Test cricket between February 1984 and June 1986, a long period of potential anxiety and self-appraisal. But the time was well used. He played county cricket again in 1985 and then set off for a winter with Natal, in South Africa, where his action and attitude were improved. He came back looking much more the complete article, the run-up more controlled in its rhythmical acceleration, the delivery stride still spectacularly long but the end result more consistent. He still bowled fast, sometimes very fast, but he had learned to unsettle batsmen by changes of pace and angle, too.

HIGHLIGHTS 🏆

Graham Dilley was only 21 when Clive Lloyd, guru to the West Indian machine, labelled him the fastest white bowler in the world and predicted a great future for him. Lloyd had just survived a furiously hostile spell from Dilley on a quick Jamaica pitch in the 1981 series. More than seven years on, retired as a player but still closely involved, Lloyd sat on the West Indian balcony at Lord's as Dilley set about fulfilling his forecast.

The West Indian batsmen had maintained a healthy respect for Dilley ever since 1981 but the effects of his back injury meant that he missed the next two series against them. As England lost them both 5–0 he might not have been heartbroken but in 1988, although the gulf between the teams remained, Dilley at least provided England with some heavy artillery to set against the West Indian quick bowlers.

It was on the first morning of the second Test at Lord's that Dilley enjoyed the sort of purple patch every fast bowler dreams about. The early sunshine had given way to a low, hazy cloud, promoting lavish swing. Dilley was well equipped to use it. Several times, in his opening burst, he beat Haynes with the outswinger before cleverly altering his line to have him caught at short-leg. Then, in his eighth, ninth and tenth overs he produced perfect awayswingers to dismiss Greenidge, Richardson and the great Richards. He had taken four for 24 and continued to roar in with four slips and two gullies crouching in rare anticipation. The huge crowd at Lord's loved it. The West Indies were getting some of their own medicine.

Maybe it was too good to last. True, Dilley finished with five for 55, and match figures of nine for 128, but the West Indies had their match-winner in Malcolm Marshall. For all that, the effort was not wasted. Those who were at Lord's on that Thursday morning saw a session to live in the memory, and a blond-haired hero straight out of comic books.

Dilley is not the type to respond to such a description. Unlike his county team-mate Ian Botham, he is not the stuff of film stars and TV celebrities. A quiet, family man, as different from his rampaging fast-bowler's image as it is possible to imagine, Dilley happily retreats from the spotlight rather than seeking it. His bowling, however, has served England well on many occasions during the 1980s and if he had possessed a consistent partner, as Trueman had Statham and Lillee had Thomson, England's recent record in Test cricket might have looked markedly more impressive.

JOHN EMBUREY

RECORD

John Ernest Emburey was born in Peckham, south London on 20 August 1952. An off-spin bowler, 6 feet 2 inches tall and sturdily built, he began his county career with Surrey before being offered terms by rivals Middlesex. He made his debut in 1973 but it was another four years before he won a cap and a regular place. He took 103 wickets in 1983 and, as vice-captain, has played a large part in Middlesex's consistent success. Since 1978, when he played his first Test, he has been England's number one off-spinner and, during 1988, he led his country in two Tests. He has now played more than 50 Tests, plus a similar number of one-day internationals.

❝ I like to use my control to put pressure on the batsmen, react to what he does and force him into error ❞

John Emburey

TECHNIQUE

A spinner can suffer just as acutely as a pace bowler from loss of rhythm, and it can be, at its worst, a painful sight. In recent years there have been various examples of slow bowlers whose action and delivery have become no better than a joke, simply through a plunge in confidence. Emburey's luck has never been quite so low but he did go through a spell where he ceased to believe in his bowling, stopped taking wickets and became, consequently, a shadow of the man generally regarded as the finest off-spinner in the world.

Like every professional worth his salt, Emburey fretted over his problems, examined the possible causes and gradually eliminated the defects. Sometimes, this kind of nightmare can literally be cured over-night, by an unwitting change in the delivery stride and a sudden infusion of confidence. More often, it needs some dedicated work.

The off-spinner at the point of delivery, the spinning fingers about to be pulled across the ball, and (right) perfectly balanced in the aftermath as the ball loops out of the hand

At his best, Emburey is a spinner fit for the coaching manual. His height is an advantage and he makes the best use of it. His left arm acts as the sighter, his left shoulder points classically down the pitch and his right arm comes over very high.

He is not a dramatically big spinner of the ball, being conditioned by the surfeit of limited-overs bowling into a style which relies more on subtle changes of flight and direction, at which he has few peers.

HIGHLIGHTS

England's cricketing stock rose several points in the winter of 1986–7. Under Mike Gatting's forceful, developing captaincy, the Ashes series was won 2–1 in Australia, where England also triumphed in two limited-overs competitions. It was a winter of heady success, so it is ironical that the most riveting match, one featuring heroics by John Emburey, ended in defeat.

The Ashes had already been safely retained when the two teams arrived at Sydney for the final Test. This did not entirely deter the Australian public, almost 100,000 people turning up to see a game which held everyone's attention up to the penultimate over.

Things did not begin well for Emburey. Australia totalled 343 in their first innings and, like the other England bowlers, he suffered heavily against the batting of Dean Jones, who scored 184 not out. England were in dire trouble at 142 for six when Emburey came in to bat. Soon, he was hobbling with a strained groin but, biting on the bullet, he stayed three and a half hours to score 69 and keep England in the hunt. Then came his greatest contribution to an epic Test Match. As Australia tried to build an impregnable position, Emburey wheeled through 46 overs of controlled spin bowling. From 106 for two, Australia were bowled out for 251, with Emburey responsible for the last seven wickets.

Now, the hunt was on. A target of 320 was undoubtedly stiff but Gatting scored a brave 96 and Emburey batted more than an hour for 22. The prospect of victory vanished with Gatting's dismissal but England still looked like holding out until Emburey's efforts were laid to waste by a grubber which bowled him with only an over left. It was Australia's first win in 15 Tests and the 13,000 last day crowd went home happy. They also took home a memory of an Englishman who did not know the meaning of defeat until finally it was forced upon him.

Neil Foster

Record 📖

Neil Alan Foster was born at Colchester, Essex on 6 May 1962. A right-arm fast-medium bowler, he was called into the Essex team for his Championship debut in 1980, while still at school. His headmaster had to grant permission for him to miss lessons. His career was seriously threatened by a back injury which required major surgery but he made a complete recovery and was chosen for England in 1983. He has played a leading role in the Essex successes of recent years and is now an established and respected member of the England team, approaching his peak. The best figures of his career are eight for 107 in the Leeds Test against Pakistan in 1987.

' Instead of concentrating on raw pace, Foster has developed some subtler skills '

Technique 🏏

In the early 1980s, England were crying out for fast bowling talent. Bob Willis was nearing the end of his career and, apart from the still immature Graham Dilley, there was no replacement in sight. So the excitement which greeted the appearance of a lanky East Anglian teenager was understandable and justified. Neil Foster looked to have a big future ahead of him and, despite regular setbacks, he has begun to fulfil the highest expectations.

At first, Foster hinted he would become a fast bowler in the true tradition. His run-up was smooth and purposeful, his action delightfully high. Even as an 18-year-old rookie in county cricket, he was hurrying good batsmen.

In this respect, he has been a surprise, though not an unpleasant one. Instead of concentrating on raw pace, Foster has developed some subtler skills. He brings the ball down sharply from his 6 feet 4 inches and, when pitch conditions are suitable, he moves it either way off the seam at a speed quite sharp enough to disturb. He has shortened his run-up in recent years and improved his control, so that he now wastes very few deliveries. He has also improved his physical strength and stamina to enable him to bowl long spells.

The follow-through should never be neglected by a budding fast bowler. The bowling arm is pulled down across the body, but the vital balance is maintained

HIGHLIGHTS 🏆

In sport, as in life itself, heroics are all too often performed in vain. In Neil Foster's case, this is especially true. He chose the Third Test of 1987 to produce his most inspiring bowling – yet it coincided with such a dismal display by the rest of the England team, that Pakistan romped to victory by an innings, the only positive result in the five-match series.

England failed to reach 200 in either innings, the brilliance of Imran's bowling matched, it seemed, by the batsmen's suspicions of a Leeds pitch which had recently brought them nothing but misfortune. The rout, however, could not detract from Foster's marvellous marathon.

England had been dismissed by tea on the first day, so Foster was quickly in action. He had taken the first two Pakistan wickets before stumps that night and, although the second day was primarily taken up with Pakistan building a big lead, Foster continued to wave the England flag. He took all the first six wickets, at which point everyone began gossiping on the possibility of him taking all ten – a feat which only Jim Laker, in the famous Old Trafford Test of 1956, has ever achieved, at international level.

In the end, Foster fell two short, but his figures of eight for 107 were still a glowing tribute to his fighting qualities as much as his skill, while the fact that he bowled no fewer than 46.2 overs said a great deal about his fitness and determination.

Being a fiercely competitive team man, Foster would not have been consoled by his personal figures, amid the depression of such a crushing defeat, but in years to come he will look back on the game with a sense of pride. He may also feel a slight sense of wonder, for at two stages of his teens it began to seem unlikely he would ever have the chance for such heroics. Stress fractures of his spine forced him to have two six-inch metal plates inserted in his back; no one could be sure if he would ever bowl again. Even before then, his sporting intentions had been confused by a football trial with Ipswich Town. Their manager was Bobby Robson, now in charge of England, and for a time Foster was torn between two games. We think he made the right choice.

JOEL GARNER

RECORD 📖

Joel Garner was born on the island of Barbados on 16 December 1952. A right-arm fast bowler, immensely tall at 6 feet 8 inches, he first played for Barbados in 1976 and for the West Indies a year later. His first series, at home to Pakistan, brought him 25 wickets, including eight in one match at Georgetown. Against Australia, the following year, he had taken 13 wickets in the first two Tests before his links with Packer cost him his place. Once the split was healed, he held a regular place in the West Indies side until his retirement in 1987, his 58 Tests producing 259 wickets at a remarkable average of 20.97. Brilliantly effective in limited-overs cricket, he played with great success for Somerset between 1977 and 1986.

‘ They should cut him off at the knees to make him bowl at a normal height ’

Geoff Boycott, 1981

TECHNIQUE 🏏

Although he was not the quickest bowler of his time, Joel Garner was commonly thought to be the most awkward customer to bat against. One of the tallest cricketers in Test history, he combined rhythmical control with appreciable pace and bounce.

Men as large as Garner, of which there are not very many, could be expected to suffer from clumsy coordination. There was not a hint of it in the bowling of this likeable, smiling Bajan. He used an economically short run-up but not a stride of it was wasted. Broad-shouldered, and with exceptionally long arms, he exaggerated his gifts with a high action which, on some grounds, meant that in the batsman's line of sight the ball was actually being delivered from above the sightscreen, an unwelcome additional hazard.

Garner could bowl in long spells, either with the new ball or as first change, and although he occasionally produced a snorting bouncer with no visible change in action, his most devastating ball was the yorker, fired in at the batsman's boots and gaining him a remarkable number of victims. As he also had a fine control of swing, could move the ball sideways off the seam and change his pace at will, it can be seen that a batsman's skill and concentration were put to a stern test by any meeting with Garner.

HIGHLIGHTS ♈

Those who have to confine their cricket-watching to the big occasions at Lord's will vividly recall 1979 as Garner's year. Twice, in ten weeks, the giant West Indian came to headquarters for a cup final and won it with a destructive, dramatic spell of bowling. At the end of it all, the West Indies had retained the World Cup and Somerset, his adopted county, had won the Gillette Cup for the first time.

Garner had not played in the inaugural World Cup in 1975 but the competition suited him. Twelve overs, with economy as important as wicket-taking, presented no problems. The problems were entirely in the court of the batsmen, who could not afford simply to survive – they had to score runs. In the 1979 final, England provided the opposition. Underdogs, of course, their chances were slim even before Garner played his hand. A marvellous century from Viv Richards had carried the West Indies to a formidable score of 286 for nine. Although Geoff Boycott and Mike Brearley, the captain, bravely saw off the initial onslaught from Roberts and Holding and took their opening stand to 129, England were well behind the asking rate. The middle order men needed to accelerate and who should be in their path but the man they call 'Big Bird'.

Garner ruthlessly plucked out the stroke-makers who just might have made a match of it. He clean-bowled Gooch for 32 and both Gower and Larkins for nought. With Botham falling to Colin Croft for only four,

England were powerless to resist. Garner finished them off to complete figures of five for 38, which still stand as the best analysis in a World Cup final.

In September he was creating another record as the first bowler to take six wickets in a county knockout cup final. Somerset had waited a long time for this moment of glory. Twice, they had been beaten in the final, the second occasion only 12 months earlier, but the mighty duo of Richards and Garner ensured there was no disappointment this time. Garner's bowling had dominated the cup run. He took two for 28 against Derbyshire in the second round, five for 11 against Kent in the quarter-final and four for 24 against Middlesex to secure the return to Lord's. Crates of cider at the ready, Somerset's army of fans prepared to celebrate and their stars did not let them down. Richards smashed 117 out of 269. Northamptonshire lost three key men cheaply to Garner and never fully recovered. Garner took six for 29 although ironically, just as in the World Cup final, his compatriot Richards was adjudged Man of the Match.

RICHARD HADLEE

RECORD 📖

Richard John Hadlee was born in Christchurch, New Zealand on 3 July 1951. A right-arm fast-medium bowler, he is the son of Walter Hadlee, a Test opener turned cricket administrator, and the younger brother of Dayle Hadlee, who also played for New Zealand. He made his debut for the province of Canterbury in 1971 and was playing Test cricket a year later. He was chiefly responsible for New Zealand's first win over England in 1978, taking ten wickets in the game, and has been the catalyst for many of his country's memorable victories. He has played more than 70 Tests and is currently the leading all-time wicket-taker in Test cricket. In county cricket, he represented Nottinghamshire for ten years, doing the 'double' of 1,000 runs and 100 wickets in 1984, the first for 17 years.

❝ Many of the world's leading batsmen now regard him as the most complete new-ball bowler in the game ❞

TECHNIQUE 🏏

With his economical run-up and classical, side-on action, Richard Hadlee is an ideal model for any young fast bowler. He is 6 feet tall, though not particularly broad of build, but he uses his wiry frame to the best possible advantage. He was authentically quick in his early years but has recently sacrificed a shade of pace to add subtler skills to his bowling. Many of the world's leading batsmen now regard him as the most complete new-ball bowler in the game, his mastery of swing and seam combining with a keen cricket brain and an aggressive determination to succeed.

The key to Hadlee's success is his meticulous dedication to detail, whether concerning his own fitness and preparation or the strengths and weaknesses of opposing batsmen. He keeps records of every player he has bowled against and his calculated efforts to exploit any chinks in the armour mark him down as one of the most intelligent of modern cricketers, as respected by fellow professionals as he is admired by observers.

HIGHLIGHTS 🏆

When Richard Hadlee eventually retires and looks back on his career, it is a fair bet that his most powerful memory will be of a four-week spell, late in 1985, when he inspired the eclipse of Australia. To any New Zealand cricketer, beating the Australians had always been a pipe dream – it was something for the lofty neighbours from across the sea even to consent to play the Kiwis. Hadlee ensured that the days of an inferiority complex were long gone.

It was a three-Test series and the first match was in Brisbane, where the tropical climate can often assist seam bowlers. Day one dawned cloudy and muggy but, although Australia struggled, they reached 146 for four before the weather halted things. All four wickets had fallen to Hadlee and, the following morning, he demolished the rest of the innings in quite sensational fashion. Australia's last wickets crashed for 29 runs and Hadlee finished with nine for 52. The only wicket he missed, that of Lawson, fell to a boundary catch – by Hadlee himself.

New Zealand then piled up 553, Hadlee scoring 54, before the maestro set to work again, this time with six for 71. Australia were vanquished by an innings and 41 runs and Hadlee's match return of 15 for 123 was the best ever by a New Zealand bowler.

Australia won narrowly in Sydney, where Hadlee picked up a relatively modest seven wickets, but in the final Test at Perth he was once more unstoppable. Five wickets in the first innings and six in the second set up a New Zealand win by six wickets and left Hadlee, the undisputed man of the series, with 33 wickets from the three games, exceptional even by his own remarkable standards.

To achieve his ultimate ambition, however, Hadlee had to travel to India, a country in which he felt uncomfortable and frequently unhealthy. It was the autumn of 1988 and Hadlee had suffered frustration for nine months since breaking down in the first Test of a series against England when level with Ian Botham at the top of the wicket-taking charts. These two great all-rounders had remained locked together on 373 wickets, because Botham himself then suffered a back injury, discounting him from the 1988 Test schedule. Hadlee, fully fit again, decided to abandon his previous inhibitions about the sub-continent and returned to India in search of the elusive wicket. It was not long in coming. On the first morning of the first Test in Bangalore, Hadlee dismissed the Indian opener, Arun Lal, and went on to take four more wickets. With Botham's bowling future in doubt, the New Zealander can expect to remain number one for some time to come.

MICHAEL HOLDING

RECORD

Michael Anthony Holding was born in Kingston, Jamaica on 16 February 1954. A right-arm fast bowler, he made his debut for Jamaica at the age of 18 and was playing for the West Indies within another three years. He has played county cricket for Lancashire, in 1981, and for Derbyshire, from 1983 up to date. Tall, at 6 feet 3 inches, but sparely built in the style of a sprinter, Holding played 60 Test matches before his retirement from the highest grade in 1987. He took 249 wickets, many of them in hostile tandem with his regular new-ball partner Andy Roberts. He undertook 11 full tours for the West Indies and played 102 limited-overs internationals. A university graduate, intelligent and approachable, he remains one of the most respected figures in the game.

‘His run-up is poetical in its balance and rhythm, his delivery action is classical’

TECHNIQUE

Fast bowlers are always being advised to shorten their run-ups. In many cases the point is well made. There is no benefit to be gained from sprinting in for 30 or 35 yards if, at the point of delivery, the action is flawed. There is also no point in running in almost as quickly as one can propel the ball, as sometimes seems to be the case. But, despite all the talk of slow over-rates, time-wasting and lack of spin bowling, it has been rare to hear any voice raised in protest against Michael Holding.

The reason is simple enough. His run-up is poetical in its balance and rhythm, his delivery action is classical and the end result is worthy of all the build-up. At his peak, in the late 70s, Holding was awesomely fast. Even in 1981, he retained the explosive pace to beat Geoff Boycott five times in succession before smashing his stumps out of the ground with the final ball of an amazing over at Bridgetown. In later years, however, he has eased back on the throttle and concentrated on maintaining the perfect length and line while ducking the ball around in the air and off the pitch. Just occasionally, he will still be roused to bowl a spell evocative of the old express days. Always, he is worth watching and, for young bowlers, copying.

HIGHLIGHTS

The World Cup of 1975 had established the West Indies as the world's premier one-day team. But they had still to prove their mastery of the Test circuit and, the following winter, they received a shattering setback. Touring Australia in what was widely billed as the world championship series, they were crushed 5–1. Australia were at their peak, the Chappell brothers cementing the batting while Lillee, Thomson and Gilmour wreaked havoc with the ball. But they did not just win through being superior players: their discipline was crucially better. The West Indies, perhaps built up too soon into worldbeaters, let themselves down in a variety of ways and, in the Fourth Test at Sydney, Holding so lost his composure that he broke down and cried when an appeal against Ian Chappell was rejected. Holding himself, and the team as a whole, were to learn much from these reversals and, when Tony Greig prefaced the 1976 series in England with a TV interview in which, referring to events in Australia, he suggested that the West Indies could be made to 'grovel', it was all the motivation they needed.

Holding by now had already vented his frustrations of the winter on India's hapless batsmen. In the April Test on his home ground at Kingston, West Indies won by ten wickets when five Indians were unfit to bat in the second innings. Several had been struck by the explosive Holding, who took seven of the 11 wickets to fall. In England, he was to do even better, though at first controversially.

At Old Trafford in the Third Test, the first two having ended drawn, an England side containing one of the most elderly top threes in history (Edrich, Close and Steele) was terrorised by Holding. Many felt he overused the bouncer in poor light but his match figures were seven for 41 and the West Indies won at a canter. They also won the next, though only after a titanic battle at Headingley, and with the series already in the bag, the low, flat featherbed pitch at The Oval looked like providing no more than gentle practice for the batsmen. Viv Richards scored 291 on it for the West Indies, Dennis Amiss 203 for England. But in one of the most herculean fast bowling efforts ever witnessed, Holding took eight for 92 in the first innings and 14 for 149 in the match. It was a wondrous exhibition of the art of fast bowling when conditions did nothing to help and it notified the world that the West Indies were ready to dominate.

IMRAN KHAN

RECORD

Imran Khan Niazi was born in Lahore, Pakistan on 25 November 1952. A right-arm fast bowler, 6 feet tall, he was educated at Worcester Royal Grammar School and Oxford University, where he won Blues in three successive years. He played county cricket for Worcestershire from 1971 to 1976 and has since been on the Sussex staff for 12 years. He first played for Pakistan in 1971 and slowly developed into one of the world's foremost all-rounders, a high quality middle-order batsman in addition to being a potentially devastating opening bowler. He has now played more than 70 Tests for Pakistan, almost half of them as captain. Imran is the only Pakistani bowler to have taken 200 Test wickets but his total is now well above 300.

6 We didn't have any fast bowlers in Pakistan, so I used to get strange looks 9

Imran Khan

TECHNIQUE

Considering he first toured England with Pakistan as long ago as 1971, when still a schoolboy, Imran can be thought a late developing star. For it was not until he joined the World Series Cricket circuit at the end of the 70s that his potential for fast bowling was fully cultivated and, to an English audience, the extent of his talent remained hidden until the three-Test series of 1982.

Of course, everyone knew he was good, even very good. But it was in Australia, when in the pay of Kerry Packer and the company of many greats from around the cricketing globe, that Imran bloomed into the bowler rated by several leading batsmen as the most complete in the world. Video film of Imran during his early days as a Test bowler reveal an entirely different action from the one we have come to know so well.

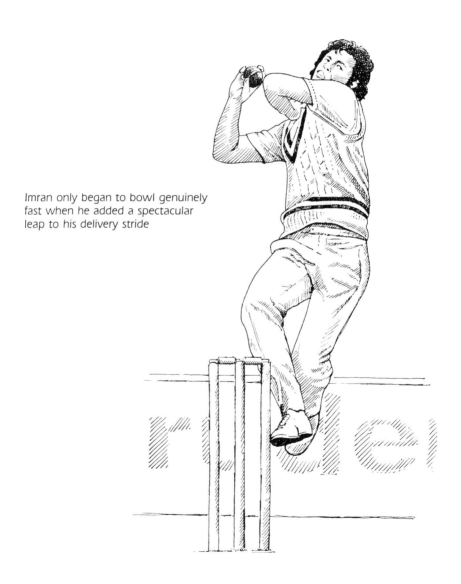

Imran only began to bowl genuinely fast when he added a spectacular leap to his delivery stride

He was predominantly an inswing bowler, short on the vital edge of pace. This was changed, during WSC, by Mike Procter and John Snow, team-mates in the glittering Rest of the World squad. Procter worked on Imran's run-up, teaching him to adopt that stooping spring now so familiar, while Snow helped him master the outswinger. At the same time, he added a spectacular leap to his delivery stride. In the heady years which followed, Imran became feared for his ferociously fast, inswinging yorkers which would trap many a man lbw, or bowled, and for the contrasting outswinger, again delivered at great speed.

HIGHLIGHTS 🏆

Pakistan cricket has long been a magnet for controversy. The recent row involving Mike Gatting and Shakoor Rana simply made front-page news of a problem which has existed for years. Nor are all the country's cricket troubles so public – Pakistan's captaincy has often changed hands like a hot potato, accompanied by seething resentment and rebellion within the dressing-room. It was from just such a situation that Imran gained the captaincy for the first time, prior to the 1982 tour of England.

It had been a busy winter for Pakistan. Under the leadership of Javed Miandad, they had been heavily beaten in two consecutive Tests in Australia before handsomely winning the Third, Imran completing a splendid series of bowling. By then, the players had evidently lost respect for Miandad and, prior to the subsequent home series against Sri Lanka, all ten who played under him in the one win over Australia refused to turn out again unless there was a promise of a change of captain for the trip to England. Seven of the ten, including Imran, missed the first two Tests with Sri Lanka but when Miandad stood down for the England series, Pakistan were able to put out a full team again. The result was a crushing defeat of the hapless Sri Lankans at Lahore. On his hometown ground, Imran was largely responsible.

He took eight for 58 in the first innings, the best figures of his Test career, and six for 58 in the second. Pakistan won by an innings and Imran, previously regarded as a cavalier with little leadership potential, was promoted to captain. What happened next is part of cricket legend. Imran proved in England that he had the tactical brain and the mental stature to provide the leadership Pakistan had often lacked. He also proved beyond doubt that he had fully matured into a masterly fast bowler.

David Lawrence

Record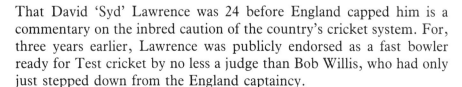

David Valentine Lawrence was born in the city of Gloucester on 28 January 1964. A right-arm fast bowler, 6 feet 3 inches tall and with the 15-stone build of a heavyweight boxer, Lawrence made his debut for Gloucestershire in 1981, playing only one match and failing to take a wicket. He again played only once in 1982 but steadily established his place and by 1985, when he took 79 Championship wickets, he was being hailed as an England fast bowler. That winter, he toured Sri Lanka with the England B team, at the same time rejecting an approach to play professional rugby league. Two moderate years followed but in 1988, his most successful season to date, he was finally chosen for England, in a Test against Sri Lanka. He was also selected for the abandoned tour to India.

‘ He became something more than a bowler who could propel the ball at outlandish pace ’

Technique

That David 'Syd' Lawrence was 24 before England capped him is a commentary on the inbred caution of the country's cricket system. For, three years earlier, Lawrence was publicly endorsed as a fast bowler ready for Test cricket by no less a judge than Bob Willis, who had only just stepped down from the England captaincy.

Willis saw in Lawrence a raw, sometimes wild but undeniably explosive bowler, capable of giving the England attack an intimidating edge. The selectors did not, apparently, agree, sending the muscular Lawrence instead on the 'reserve team' tour to Sri Lanka, where conditions were never likely to suit him.

It took Lawrence some while to make his case again, and by the time he did graduate to Test level it was with a modified run-up and action. He cut several yards off his approach, allowing greater control, and his delivery stride, though still dramatic, was not quite so uninhibited. The result was that he became something more than a bowler who could propel the ball at outlandish pace. He was making the batsmen play more often, swinging the ball and, most important, bowling longer spells than he was capable of in his early years.

At 21, Lawrence was an attractive tearaway. At 24 he was still very quick, capable of a devilish bouncer and of obtaining lift from the most docile of pitches. But he was much more the streamlined article.

HIGHLIGHTS 🏆

The romance of David Lawrence's cricketing story is not so much a single game, or a single spell of bowling, but the fact that he is there at all.

He might have become a rugby player, he might have become a boxer. He might just have exercised his passion for dancing in the discos. Instead, against the odds, he chose to pursue a fascination for cricket and, despite growing up in an underprivileged area of Gloucester and going to a school where cricket put too great a strain on the limited staff and facilities, he made it.

When, in 1988, Lawrence took 84 first-class wickets and finally earned his reward with a Test cap for England, it was all worthwhile. Lawrence, who looks extraordinarily like the British heavyweight boxer Frank Bruno, thrives on bowling. Always has done. But he has had to endure some setbacks and some jibes, certain of them very unpleasant, in his quest for glory.

He has learned to live with catcalls from ignorant spectators, however hurtful. But his resolution was put to its toughest test when, in early August 1988, injuries caused a vacancy in the England line-up for the final Test against the West Indies.

Lawrence was playing at Cheltenham at the time and his reaction to the news was to produce a spell of accurate and furiously fast bowling which brought him figures of seven for 47 against Surrey. England's selectors looked the other way and instead chose a bowler out of form and out of favour with his county. It was a kick in the teeth but what did Lawrence do? Far from sulking or giving up, he just went on bowling as much and as well as he could, until the selectors could ignore him no longer. A fast bowler's job is sometimes a taxing one, but having a heart as big as David Lawrence's is a big help.

DENNIS LILLEE

RECORD 📖

Dennis Keith Lillee was born in Perth, Western Australia on 18 July 1949, the 101st anniversary of W. G. Grace's birth. A right-arm fast bowler, the greatest of his time, Lillee burst onto the scene in 1969–70, taking 32 wickets in his first eight Sheffield Shield games for Western Australia. He made his Test debut a year later, against England, and in 1971–2 he took eight for 29 against the Rest of the World at Perth. Serious back injury followed, putting his entire career in jeopardy, but he fought back courageously and took 25 wickets in the thrashing of England in 1974–5. He played successfully in World Series Cricket but returned to the official circuit for further glories. In all, he played 70 Tests, his 355 wickets standing for some time as a world record. He played county cricket for Northamptonshire in 1988, at the age of 39.

❛There is no batsman on earth who goes out to meet Lillee and Thomson with a smile on his face❜

Clive Lloyd, 1975

TECHNIQUE 🏏

The greatest and most genuine flattery one can offer Dennis Lillee is the widespread opinion of both team-mates and opponents that he is the most complete fast bowler the game has seen, these past 20 years. There have been times, it is true, when he has outraged those who run the game, and amazed some who play it, by his arrogance and aggression but, strictly in terms of bowling, there have been few to even approach him.

Lillee had everything. A superb fast bowler's physique went hand in hand with an intimidating approach, a classical action and, for good measure, a few theatrical gestures to unsettle the batsman still further. Top of his list of virtues, however, was sheer courage. Lillee battled back from an injury which would have finished most cricketers, putting himself through agonies to regain the fanatical level of fitness he always set himself. He never was one to acknowledge a lost cause and never gave less than 100 per cent for his beloved Australia.

Later in his career, when the sharpest edge of speed was beyond him, Lillee settled sensibly for a shorter, smoother run-up, a slightly altered and more restrained action and a command of swing and seam which made him virtually as great a handful as he had been in his swaggering heyday. He played at the highest level for almost 20 years, his enthusiasm for the game never faltering, and in recent years he has willingly handed down some of his knowledge and expertise to aspiring fast bowlers both in Australia and England.

HIGHLIGHTS 🏆

The Centenary Test Match, staged at Melbourne in March 1977, was an event sure to live in the memories of all who attended. The cricket was gripping and fluctuating, while the social reunions of players old and new in the background were something to behold. The star of the show, however, was a bowler of the moment. At the end of an incredible game, Dennis Lillee was chaired from the ground by his ecstatic colleagues.

That Australia won by 45 runs – the identical result to the 1877 Test that this game celebrated – despite an innings of heroic dash and brilliance by England's clown prince Derek Randall, was due almost entirely to the magnificent Lillee. He took 11 wickets in the game, destroying England in the first innings and wearing them down in the second.

Such an outcome looked improbable when Australia were rushed out for 138 before a disbelieving first-day crowd of 61,000. England, though, fared even worse. Lillee savaged them with pace and movement, taking six for 26 as they even fell five short of 100. The organisers must have been wringing their hands. With a full programme of social events for the five scheduled days, plus enormous ticket sales, here were two teams threatening to get the game over inside two.

They need not have worried. With Rod Marsh making a century, Australia extended their lead to 462. A declaration left England the apparently impossible task of 463 in 11 hours. Randall kept the dream alive but the inexhaustible Lillee, getting through 34.4 overs, soaked up his punishment, came back for more and ultimately triumphed. It was a fitting stage for a master cricketer to enjoy perhaps his greatest hour.

MALCOLM MARSHALL

RECORD 📖

Malcolm Denzil Marshall was born in the village of St Michael, Barbados on 18 April 1958. A right-arm fast bowler, he first played for his island team in the final match of the 1977–8 Shell Shield and took six Jamaican wickets. He was chosen for the West Indies' World Cup squad in 1979, although he did not play, and in the same summer he began his county career with Hampshire, where he is still playing ten years later. In 1982, he took 134 wickets for Hampshire, the most by anyone since the reduction of the county programme in 1969. He made his Test debut against India in December 1978 although it was another five years before he laid claim to a regular place. His striking-rate during subsequent years was so extraordinary that by the end of 1988 he was fast closing on the West Indian Test record of 309 wickets, held by Lance Gibbs.

‘ He is no longer the tearaway who depends entirely on his speed to take wickets ’

TECHNIQUE 🏏

On the day Malcolm Marshall made his debut for Hampshire, in early May of 1979, flurries of snow blew into his bewildered face as he ran in to bowl. It was a strange introduction to English cricket for one brought up on the year-round sunshine of the Caribbean, but it evidently failed to bother the 21-year-old novice. Marshall took nine wickets in the game and was firmly set on a course of terrorising English batsmen, at Test and county level, for the next decade.

His adaptability is his greatest ally. Just as he adjusted to the alien weather back at Southampton ten years ago, so he has learned to frame the pace and style of his bowling to suit whatever conditions confront him. He is no longer the tearaway who depends entirely on his speed to take wickets. Although for some years he was widely thought to be the fastest bowler in the world, he can now call upon more subtle weapons. He is a master of changes in pace, slight enough to be concealed but distinct enough to confuse. He controls swing and movement off the seam better than any of his contemporaries and, when pitch

Left arm raised as a sighter, front leg about to stretch and pound down into the delivery stride – the batsman's awesome view of Marshall

conditions do not encourage outright speed, he will throttle back and go through a repertoire unequalled by any modern fast bowler. He has not acquired such skills, however, without many hours of diligent practice, a lesson which should not be lost on any who seek to emulate him.

HIGHLIGHTS

If England's main batsmen are sick of the sight of Malcolm Marshall, the plain figures will pardon them. In the past three series between the two nations, Marshall has taken 86 wickets in 14 games. His 35, during the West Indies' 4–0 victory in 1988, was arguably the high point of his career – no West Indian has ever taken more wickets in a series – but his most heroically devastating performance came four years earlier, on the Headingley ground in Leeds which seems to be the stage for so much drama.

The West Indies had won the first two Tests, by an innings and 80 runs at Edgbaston and by nine wickets at Lord's. Victory in Leeds would give them the series and Marshall did not intend to let the opportunity slip. On the opening morning, fielding in the gully to the batting of opener Chris Broad, Marshall took a crunching blow on the left thumb. A hospital examination revealed a double fracture. Doctors advised him he should play no cricket for at least ten days. Marshall thanked them and ignored them.

Back at the ground, England had been dismissed for 270, despite a century from Lamb, but the world champions' reply was not proceeding to plan. In fact, they were toiling at 206 for seven before a stand of 82 between the reliable Larry Gomes and the flamboyant Michael Holding. When Holding and Garner were out in swift succession, England assumed the innings was over. But Marshall marched out to bat one-handed, his injured thumb heavily strapped. Gomes was shepherded to his century and the West Indies passed the psychologically vital 300.

Not content with this, Marshall then joined his team-mates in the field, opened the attack and bowled furiously fast to take four wickets on the Saturday evening. Three more on the fourth morning completed figures of seven for 53, his best in Test cricket. England were dead and buried, the assassination carried out by a man who should not even have been on the field.

ABDUL QADIR

RECORD 📖

Abdul Qadir was born in Lahore, Pakistan on 15 September 1955. A leg-break and googly bowler of the highest class, Qadir plays his domestic first-class cricket for the Habib Bank side. He made his debut in 1975–6 and, two years later, took eight for 29 against Universities. That season, he was chosen for Pakistan against England and, in only his second Test, took six for 44 at Hyderabad. He had a disappointing first tour of England, in 1978, but four years on, he took 57 wickets in 12 first-class matches here. Later in 1982 he had match figures of eleven for 218 as Australia were beaten at Faisalabad. He also has match-winning spells against both the West Indies and England to his credit.

' His greatness lies in his control and variety. He is not usually a great spinner of the ball '

Imran Khan

TECHNIQUE 🏏

It is rare in cricket to find a player who is both artist and entertainer, match-winner and crowd-pleaser. Abdul Qadir, the idiosyncratic wrist-spinner, is one such precious commodity. Wherever he goes around the cricket globe, the stocky man with the mop of dark hair will enchant the crowds even if he fails to bewilder the opposition, because he injects into his bowling a joy and exuberance all too scarce in the modern game.

Qadir's bouncing approach is imitated widely, as is his instinct for theatrical gestures and appeals. What is not successfully copied is the bowling itself, genuine looping leg-spin with enough varieties to confuse and even embarrass Test-class batsmen.

The basic menu offered by the wrist-spinner is a leg-break, which turns from leg to off, and a googly which, from a very similar action, turns from off to leg. To this, Qadir adds a top-spinner, which hurries onto the unwary batsman, and a flipper, which does exactly what one would expect from the term.

He does much more than this, of course. He varies his length, pace, line and angle of delivery, using every conceivable scrap of help from the conditions and playing mercilessly on the fact that very few batsmen, these days, are at all familiar with wrist spin.

HIGHLIGHTS 🏆

The West Indies arrived in Pakistan, late in 1986, with a proud and enviable record. In the previous seven years, they had won 30 and lost only three of their 56 Tests. Few expected that record to be damaged by Imran Khan's talented but unpredictable side and yet, in the first of three Tests, played at Faisalabad, the West Indies suffered a fate nothing short of humiliation. The cause was Abdul Qadir.

There was no indication of the upset to come as Pakistan mustered only 159 in their first innings, the fast bowlers wreaking their regular havoc. West Indies took a lead of 89, despite six wickets for the emergent Wasim Akram, who then scored 66 in a Pakistan total of 328. Still, the West Indies needed only 240 in four sessions – surely well within their compass.

In the first of those four sessions, the cricket world was stood on its head. West Indies reeled into close of play at 43 for nine, Imran having taken the first two wickets before Qadir, weaving his own brand of magic as never before, destroyed the middle-order.

Supported by some brilliant close catching, Qadir had taken five for 13 in that session. The following morning, he finished the job. When he caught and bowled Marshall, he had taken six for 16 in 9.3 overs and the West Indies had been dismissed for 53, their lowest-ever score in Test cricket. Abdul Qadir has caused a lot of heartache among batsmen around the world this past decade, but this was surely his finest hour. The world champions had, if only temporarily, been dethroned.

Left: Side-on, note Qadir has a relatively short final stride and is already cocking his wrist. The batsman sees the ball emerge from the back of the hand – but will it be the leg-break or the googly?

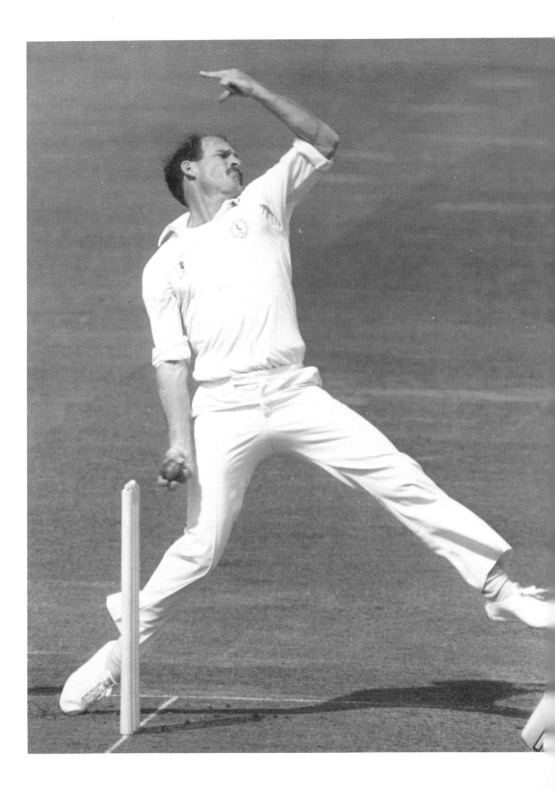

CLIVE RICE

RECORD 📖

Clive Edward Butler Rice was born in Johannesburg, South Africa on 23 July 1949. A right-arm medium-fast bowler, and a splendid high-order batsman, Rice made his debut for his native province of Transvaal in 1969 and has now been playing for them for 20 years, the last eight as captain. In England, he joined Nottinghamshire in 1975 and spent 13 seasons at Trent Bridge. He captained them between 1979 and 1987, taking them to two county championships and to the NatWest Trophy. Deprived of Test cricket by South Africa's isolation, he has been an inspirational all-rounder in two countries' domestic cricket. He also led South Africa in unofficial 'Tests' against West Indian and Australian teams, taking a hat-trick against the Australians in Johannesburg.

'He emerged as unarguably one of the world's premier all-rounders'

TECHNIQUE

As his 40th birthday began to loom ever nearer, Clive Rice undertook less and less bowling. He retired from English cricket after the 1987 season but continued to play for Transvaal and, still remarkably fit, he finished fifth in the Currie Cup bowling averages (as well as third in the batting) during the 1987–8 season. Being above all else a sensibly dedicated cricketer, however, Rice was now looking after himself, bowling in shorter spells and at a pace much reduced from ten and even 15 years earlier.

At that time, he had been undeniably sharp. His slightly swaggering run-up, climaxed by a leap and a whirling action, could be tailored to suit all conditions but he was at his most effective on the green, seaming pitches seen so often at Trent Bridge. On such a surface, he would hit the seam with mechanical consistency, whipping the ball into or away from the batsman at a lively speed.

Rice has so many facets to his game. A calm, correct and accomplished batsman, superbly safe slip catcher and wise, influential captain, his strongest suit is hard to define. Perhaps it is enough to say that if South Africa had been playing Test cricket for the past 20 years, Rice would have been taking the new ball more often than not.

HIGHLIGHTS 🏆

From all the memories in his prolonged and productive career in two countries, Clive Rice may well choose the English summer of 1981 as the period in which he emerged as unarguably one of the world's premier all-rounders. In years to come he was twice to win competitions designed to find the best all-round cricketer in the world, and he was to lead his native country with some success. But it was as captain of Nottinghamshire, a job he had earned, lost and then reclaimed, that he proved himself to be someone special.

Rice had first been appointed to lead the county side in 1978. Then, when it was discovered that he had signed a contract with World Series Cricket, he was sacked from the job and released from the staff. A compromise agreement brought him back into the fold, but not as captain, and it was late the following season before he was again offered the position. When he did take over, the change effected an instant improvement in the county's fortunes. They rose to third in the County Championship in 1980; the following season, they won the title for the first time in 52 years and Rice, in conjunction with the great Richard Hadlee, had much to do with it.

During that memorable summer, Rice scored more than 1,400 runs and, in the Championship alone, took 65 wickets at under 20 runs apiece. More important still, he struck when it was most needed. In August, Nottinghamshire faced a vital game with Surrey, who were then second in the table. Rice brushed them aside, taking nine wickets in the game, including six for 44 in the second innings. He was just as effective in limited-overs cricket and, as Notts went through the group stages of the Benson and Hedges Cup unbeaten, Rice included match-winning figures of six for 22 against Northants.

Both Rice and Nottinghamshire went on to further glories in subsequent years. But it was that summer of 1981 when their relationship produced seriously successful returns.

RAVI SHASTRI

RECORD 📖

Ravishankar Jayadritha Shastri was born in Bombay, India on 27 May 1962. A left-arm spin bowler, tall and slim, he made his debut for Bombay in 1979 and played his first Test Match when only 18 years old. He took 15 wickets in his first three Tests and has not often been omitted from the India side since then. He captained India's Under-19 side in 1980–1, and was a member of the World Cup-winning squad in 1983, although he did not play in the final. With more than 2,500 runs and approaching 150 wickets he is now a genuine Test all-rounder and, late in 1987, captained India temporarily. He has played county cricket for Glamorgan since 1987.

' Shastri is of a different breed to many of his predecessors – he is a modern '

TECHNIQUE

One of the latest in a long line of successful Indian spin bowlers, Ravi Shastri is of a different breed to many of his predecessors. Whereas Bishen Bedi, the turbaned artist of the 1970s, typified his age with looping, flighted spin, Shastri is a modern. Conditioned by the heavy demands on economy in one-day cricket Shastri's natural style is to bowl flat and relatively fast, concentrating on the batsman's pads and, unless the ball is turning, operating to a leg-side field.

He is extremely accurate and, at 6 feet 3 inches, brings the ball down from a decent height to assist extra bounce. When conditions are helpful he will slow down his bowling, give the ball more air and strive for turn, but on the sort of pitches encountered in Test cricket these days, he does not often have the opportunity. Shastri has a smooth, high action and has been India's senior spinner for some years.

HIGHLIGHTS 🏆

To say that Ravi Shastri's Test career had an eventful start would be a hopeless understatement. Still only 18, he was playing in a domestic fixture in Bombay when a telephone call came through from New Zealand, where the Indian team were touring. Dilip Doshi, the regular left-arm spinner, was injured and Shastri was to catch the first plane out.

He arrived in the windy city of Wellington on the eve of the First Test, to be told he was in the side. With Geoff Howarth scoring an unbeaten century, the home team amassed a big total but Shastri responded gamely to the pressure and took three wickets.

His first Test Match innings was a humble affair, at number ten. In years to come, he was to bat in every other position, bar eleven, for his country. Even this did not go without a hitch, however, for his first scoring shot resulted in the run-out of his partner as they attempted a fourth run!

The match took another twist when New Zealand, 152 ahead on first innings, collapsed spectacularly. They were 99 for seven when Shastri began a new over. At the end of it, they were 100 all out, the new young spin king having taken three wickets in four deliveries. It was not enough to bring India victory – they still lost by 62 runs – but it was quite enough excitement to be going on with. Two matches later Shastri, having retained his place despite Doshi's return, bowled 56 overs in the New Zealand first innings at Auckland and took five for 125. His Test career was properly launched.

JEFF THOMSON

RECORD 📖

Jeffrey Robert Thomson was born in Sydney, Australia on 16 August 1950. A right-arm fast bowler, he made his debut for his native New South Wales in 1972 but transferred to Queensland, where he now lives, two years later. Thrown into the 1974–5 series against England by selectors gambling that his one previous Test appearance was best forgotten, he was a sensation, taking 33 wickets at 17.93 apiece and forming the immortal new-ball pairing with Dennis Lillee. Although often troubled by shoulder injuries he went on to play 51 times for Australia, taking exactly 200 wickets. He played one season of county cricket, for Middlesex in 1981, and retired after taking 42 wickets in his final Sheffield Shield season in 1985–6.

‘ Thommo was a one-off, and none the worse for that **’**

TECHNIQUE

Despite playing Test cricket over a period of ten years, Jeff Thomson will be remembered for his awesome deeds in a three-year span during the mid-1970s when, in sequence, he helped devastate the English and West Indian batting before bolstering Australia's ailing resources when Kerry Packer's chequebook ravaged them.

Thomson had no great depth or subtlety to his bowling. He was simply very quick, nothing more and nothing less. His action bore more resemblance to a javelin thrower than a fast bowler from the coaching manual, his right arm emerging from behind his back in a dramatic final twist to an explosive slinging delivery.

He was literally a beach boy before cricket claimed him, soaking up the sun along the Sydney coastline and surfing for sport. He was immensely strong, an asset which became significant as he rampaged through England's batting in 1974–5, often achieving quite uncanny and frightening lift from a good length.

His unconventional action inevitably took its toll on his body and such contortions are not to be recommended to anyone who wants to survive as a bowler. Thommo was a one-off, and none the worse for that.

HIGHLIGHTS

Considering he is an extremely pleasant, fairly quiet and easy-going man, Jeff Thomson evokes a wide variety of sharp, painful and hostile memories among the Test batsmen of the 1970s. The England team who came up against him at Brisbane in November of 1974, scarcely having heard of him before, will hardly wish to recall the episode at all. Thomson took nine wickets and caused an awful lot of bruises. The West Indian side at Sydney a year later suffered similar indignities against this raw, high-powered express. But for sheer spectacular speed, this time against the odds, it can be said that an evening at Kensington Oval in Barbados, during the spring of 1978, brought Thomson's finest hour.

He had gone to the Caribbean with virtually an Australian reserve side, most of the stars having joined up with World Series Cricket. Thomson, who initially signed for Packer but then withdrew, was the star in a strange mix of a side captained by the veteran Bob Simpson. The West Indies by contrast, were at full strength and predictably won the first Test by an innings.

Barbados hosted the next Test and Australia were in trouble again. All out for 250 soon after tea on the first day, they had just over an hour to retrieve something. Thomson rose superbly to the challenge. He sprinted in like a man inspired and if he has ever bowled faster, heaven help those who faced him.

There has always been a touch of the rebel in Thomson (when he finished his cricket career, for instance, he turned his back on all media or coaching opportunities to start a gardening operation) and it was rebellion, of a kind, which provoked this vintage piece of cricket. Thomson did not like being a loser and, in this series, he could see he was on a hiding to nothing. His furious reaction was such a spectacle that even the partisan Bajan crowd roared him in to the wicket.

During that unforgettable hour, he dismissed Greenidge, Richards and Kallicharran. Two were caught off the glove from rising balls and Richards who, typically, had taken on Thomson with a flurry of hooks and pulls, perished to a catch at long-leg. Haynes and Lloyd survived, but only just, and despite final figures of six for 77 for Thomson, the West Indies went on to win comfortably. None of their players, however, will ever forget that magical hour of a man bowling as fast as is humanly possible.

DEREK UNDERWOOD

RECORD

Derek Leslie Underwood was born in Brömley, Kent on 8 June 1945. A left-arm slow bowler he made his debut for Kent at the age of 17 and became the youngest player in history to take 100 first-class wickets in his first season. He achieved the feat on nine further occasions in a county career spanning 25 years, and in 1966 he took a remarkable 157. He was chosen for England, against the West Indies, when just 21 years old and went on to play 86 Tests, despite interrupting his international career to play World Series cricket and terminating it with a disapproved trip to South Africa. His 297 Test wickets are included in a career total of 2,465, taken at just 20 runs apiece. He was awarded the MBE in 1981.

‘A master of variations in pace and slight shifts in angle’

TECHNIQUE

To describe Derek Underwood as a slow bowler, or simply as a spinner, is to give a false picture of a unique performer. Much of his bowling was actually delivered at a respectable medium pace, and always off a plodding run-up of ten yards or so. When conditions were right he would turn the ball extravagantly, but on good pitches, against good players, he would still take plentiful wickets through his unfailing accuracy. Batsmen, infuriated or entranced by the unhittable length and line firing at them with the remorseless regularity of a bowling machine, would very often commit cricketing suicide in their frustration.

Underwood was at his most effective on the uncovered English pitches of the sixties and early seventies. On a 'sticky dog' – the cricket slang for a pitch affected by rain – he could be unplayable. Full covering failed to thwart him, however, and both in county and Test cricket he maintained a high success rate through his dedicated attention to detail. A bad delivery from Underwood was a rarity and the anguish over it would be etched on his expresssion.

Although sometimes accused of bowling a negative, flat trajectory

Rhythm is the key to the Underwood machine, perfectly oiled and apparently unvaried, but concealing some cunning changes of pace and angle

when conditions demanded something more flighted, Underwood was a master of variations in pace and slight shifts in angle. He won countless lbw victims with the ball which swung into the right-hander, 'with the arm'.

HIGHLIGHTS

Derek Underwood's most memorable triumph, of many in his long career, was to retrieve a series against Australia which had seemed hopelessly lost. The circumstances of the story are extraordinary and the fact that they could not be repeated now makes it a tale worth retelling.

It was 1968 and England, captained by Colin Cowdrey, had lost the first Test to Bill Lawry's Australians and then drawn the next three. Underwood, who did not play in the defeat, bowled creditably in each succeeding game, but his hour of glory arrived literally at the last gasp.

The final Test, played as tradition demands at The Oval, had been dictated by England. They gained a first-innings lead of 170 and, although England were dismissed second time around for 181, Australia looked doomed when they went into lunch on the fifth day at 86 for five. Their salvation then seemed to arrive with a violent thunderstorm, which left the pitch and surrounds completely flooded. Further play looked to be out of the question but when the sun reappeared, the groundstaff were joined by volunteers from the crowd in a frantic mopping-up operation. To Australia's dismay, the game resumed at 4.45 p.m. England had 15 minutes, plus a final, desperate hour, in which to take five wickets and square the series.

For 40 minutes they were denied. Then, with time and hope fast diminishing, D'Oliveira made the breakthrough. It was now 110 for six. Half an hour later, Australia were all out for 125, Underwood having taken the remaining four wickets to clinch the victory with just five minutes to spare. Cowdrey had recalled him immediately after the fall of the sixth wicket and, using the unusual conditions brilliantly, he baffled each batsman in turn. Finally, with every England fielder camped around the bat, opener John Inverarity, who had batted through the innings for 56, played no shot to Underwood's famous inswinging 'arm ball' and was out lbw. The crowd celebrated in style, while television viewers could scarcely credit the half-hour of gripping sporting drama they had just witnessed.

Bob Willis

Record

Robert George Dylan Willis was born on 30 May 1949 in Sunderland. A right-arm fast bowler, 6 feet 6 inches tall, he made his county debut for Surrey in 1969 but left them two years later to play for Warwickshire, where he stayed until retirement in 1984. He first played for England in Australia on the 1970–1 tour, flown out in mid-series as an emergency replacement, and in all he played 90 Tests, taking 325 wickets at 25 runs apiece. He made 11 full England tours, plus another as assistant manager, but the high point of his long career came at Headingley in 1981, with a match-winning spell of eight for 43 against Australia.

> **'** I had been in cricket for ten years before I realized what a bizarre run-up I possessed **'**
>
> Bob Willis

Technique

Being a disarmingly modest man, Bob Willis openly confesses that he has no idea how he survived for so long as England's premier fast bowler with so many apparent defects in his method. His run-up, all flailing arms and legs, was once described as a 'broken-down biplane', while his open-chested delivery makes the purist coaches wince and puts persistent stress on Willis's rakish frame. In textbook terms, he does almost everything wrong, so how can his remarkable record be explained?

The reasons are these. He was always able to bowl fast naturally, he kept himself very fit by punishing training routines and he was sustained through good times and bad by a single-minded determination matched by few other sportsmen of his time.

If there is little to recommend to the aspiring fast bowler about Willis's action, his attitude to the game could profitably be copied by anyone wishing to advance. Willis was a chronic worrier and an insomniac at big-match times so he even enlisted the help of a hypnotherapist who, he relates, taught him greater self-belief. While this may be too extreme a method for most, Willis's dedicated training, pre-match preparation both in the nets and exercise routines, stamina and endless enthusiasm for bowling are the qualities which made him great.

HIGHLIGHTS 🏆

Whether he likes it or not, Bob Willis will forever be primarily remembered for Headingley, 1981. He is personally convinced that he has more than once bowled better than he did on that unforgettable Yorkshire day without taking a single wicket but history's love of the dramatic has no time for such sentiments. At Headingley, Willis's bowling won a Test Match against Australia which had evidently been beyond salvage before Ian Botham's spectacular innings and still looked almost irretrievable when, in pursuit of only 130 to win, the Australians reached 56 for one.

It was then that Willis persuaded Mike Brearley, the England captain, to take a decision which altered the course of the series. Willis had been toiling uphill and into the wind from the football stand end at Leeds. By his own admission, he had been bowling poorly. As a final shot, he asked to change ends. Brearley, running out of options, agreed, and Willis dismissed Australia for 111 with a staggering spell of inspired fast bowling.

He took eight of the last nine wickets, helped by some superb catching but forcing the errors through tight control of length and line on a pitch giving a certain amount of assistance. Through it all, Willis's face was a strange mask of stressful concentration, almost trancelike in its intensity.

Part of the reason for this was only revealed much later. Willis believed he would be dropped if he did not produce something worthwhile in that Australian innings. He had taken nought for 72 in the first innings, bowling without his usual zip, and the selectors must by then have been grimly accepting they had made a mistake. For, although it was never made public, Willis was not even selected for the Test which now stands as his bowling epitaph. He had missed some cricket through a heavy cold and Brearley, in consultation with the selection panel, had decided they did not want a half-fit bowler for so vital a game. When Willis was informed by telephone, he literally talked his way back into the team before it could be officially announced. On that slender thread hung a slice of cricket history.

CAREER RECORDS

First-class figures are to end of the 1988 English season; Test figures
are to 7 February 1989.

T. M. Alderman

First-class

	Balls	Runs	Wickets	Average	5w/inns	10w/match
			711	23.72	39	7

Test cricket

	Balls	Runs	Wickets	Average	5w/inns	10w/match
v. England	2208	982	43	22.83	4	–
v. New Zealand	707	311	8	38.87	–	–
v. Pakistan	782	406	10	40.60	–	–
v. West Indies	1676	903	18	50.16	1	–
TOTAL	5373	2597	79	32.87	5	–

I. T. Botham

First-class

	Balls	Runs	Wickets	Average	5w/inns	10w/match
			1005	26.84	53	7

Test cricket

	Balls	Runs	Wickets	Average	5w/inns	10w/match
v. Australia	7999	3852	145	26.56	9	2
v. India	3371	1558	59	26.40	6	1
v. New Zealand	3152	1424	61	23.34	6	1
v. Pakistan	2347	1210	40	30.25	2	–
v. Sri Lanka	485	269	10	26.90	1	–
v. West Indies	3447	2079	58	35.84	3	–
TOTAL	20801	10392	373	27.86	27	4

S. T. Clarke

First-class

	Balls	Runs	Wickets	Average	5w/inns	10w/match
			920	19.38	58	10

Test cricket

	Balls	Runs	Wickets	Average	5w/inns	10w/match
v. Australia	486	217	7	31.00	–	–
v. India	1403	711	21	33.85	1	–
v. Pakistan	588	242	14	17.28	–	–
TOTAL	2477	1170	42	27.85	1	–

Kapil Dev

First-class

	Balls	Runs	Wickets	Average	5w/inns	10w/match
			658	26.99	32	3

Test cricket

	Balls	Runs	Wickets	Average	5w/inns	10w/match
v. Australia	3042	1358	54	25.14	5	–
v. England	5267	2596	71	36.56	4	–
v. New Zealand	1170	487	18	27.05	–	–
v. Pakistan	4932	2604	87	29.93	7	1
v. Sri Lanka	1590	810	28	28.92	1	–
v. West Indies	3758	1831	71	25.78	2	1
TOTAL	19759	9686	329	29.44	19	2

G. R. Dilley

First-class

	Balls	Runs	Wickets	Average	5w/inns	10w/match
			548	25.96	26	2

Test cricket

	Balls	Runs	Wickets	Average	5w/inns	10w/match
v. Australia	2156	1031	36	28.63	1	–
v. India	1142	649	17	38.17	–	–
v. New Zealand	1196	441	24	18.37	2	–
v. Pakistan	1149	632	20	31.60	2	–
v. West Indies	2039	1036	36	28.77	1	–
TOTAL	7682	3789	133	28.48	6	–

J. E. Emburey

First-class

	Balls	Runs	Wickets	Average	5w/inns	10w/match
			1092	25.23	52	8

Test cricket

	Balls	Runs	Wickets	Average	5w/inns	10w/match
v. Australia	6396	2206	67	32.92	3	–
v. India	1055	363	10	36.30	–	–
v. New Zealand	1457	417	9	46.33	–	–
v. Pakistan	1386	473	7	67.57	–	–
v. Sri Lanka	384	126	7	18.00	1	–
v. West Indies	2637	1178	30	39.26	2	–
TOTAL	13315	4763	130	36.63	6	–

N. A. Foster

First-class

	Balls	Runs	Wickets	Average	5w/inns	10w/match
			578	24.11	34	6

Test cricket

	Balls	Runs	Wickets	Average	5w/inns	10w/match
v. Australia	342	137	3	45.66	–	–
v. India	900	427	18	23.72	2	1
v. New Zealand	882	373	6	62.16	–	–
v. Pakistan	1580	673	28	24.03	2	–
v. Sri Lanka	324	149	5	29.80	–	–
v. West Indies	1051	617	16	38.56	1	–
TOTAL	5079	2376	76	31.26	5	1

J. Garner

First-class

	Balls	Runs	Wickets	Average	5w/inns	10w/match
			881	18.53	48	7

Test cricket

	Balls	Runs	Wickets	Average	5w/inns	10w/match
v. Australia	4190	1860	89	20.89	4	–
v. England	4428	1650	92	17.93	1	–
v. India	678	301	7	43.60	–	–
v. New Zealand	2013	742	36	20.61	2	–
v. Pakistan	1860	880	35	25.14	–	–
TOTAL	13169	5433	259	20.97	7	–

R. J. Hadlee

First-class

	Balls	Runs	Wickets	Average	5w/inns	10w/match
			1413	18.00	96	17

Test cricket

	Balls	Runs	Wickets	Average	5w/inns	10w/match
v. Australia	5851	2565	123	20.88	13	3
v. England	5050	2015	81	24.87	7	2
v. India	2471	1174	53	22.15	4	2
v. Pakistan	2457	1279	46	27.80	4	–
v. Sri Lanka	1405	473	37	12.78	2	1
v. West Indies	2506	1124	51	22.03	4	1
TOTAL	19740	8630	391	22.08	34	9

M. A. Holding

First-class

	Balls	Runs	Wickets	Average	5w/inns	10w/match
			740	23.11	38	4

Test cricket

	Balls	Runs	Wickets	Average	5w/inns	10w/match
v. Australia	3774	1771	76	23.30	5	1
v. England	4486	2031	96	21.15	6	1
v. India	3142	1543	61	25.26	2	–
v. New Zealand	1278	553	16	34.56	–	–
TOTAL	12680	5898	249	23.68	13	2

Imran Khan

First-class

	Balls	Runs	Wickets	Average	5w/inns	10w/match
			1255	21.86	70	13

Test cricket

	Balls	Runs	Wickets	Average	5w/inns	10w/match
v. Australia	3574	1431	60	23.85	3	1
v. England	2919	1158	47	24.63	4	1
v. India	3965	1756	81	21.67	6	2
v. New Zealand	1571	676	24	28.16	1	–
v. Sri Lanka	1734	657	46	14.28	3	1
v. West Indies	3374	1641	76	21.59	6	1
TOTAL	17137	7319	334	21.91	23	6

D. V. Lawrence

First-class

	Balls	Runs	Wickets	Average	5w/inns	10w/match
			331	33.25	14	–

Test cricket

	Balls	Runs	Wickets	Average	5w/inns	10w/match
v. Sri Lanka	216	111	3	37.00	–	–
TOTAL	216	111	3	37.00	–	–

D. K. Lillee

First-class

	Balls	Runs	Wickets	Average	5w/inns	10w/match
			882	23.46	50	13

Test cricket

	Balls	Runs	Wickets	Average	5w/inns	10w/match
v. England	8516	3507	167	21.00	11	4
v. India	891	452	21	21.52	–	–
v. New Zealand	1770	740	38	19.47	4	1
v. Pakistan	4433	2160	71	30.42	5	1
v. Sri Lanka	180	107	3	35.66	–	–
v. West Indies	2677	1526	55	27.74	3	1
TOTAL	18467	8493	355	23.92	23	7

M. D. Marshall

First-class

	Balls	Runs	Wickets	Average	5w/inns	10w/match
			1210	17.89	70	10

Test cricket

	Balls	Runs	Wickets	Average	5w/inns	10w/match
v. Australia	3397	1522	66	23.06	7	1
v. England	4403	1862	104	17.90	6	1
v. India	2839	1381	57	24.23	3	–
v. New Zealand	1735	775	36	21.53	1	1
v. Pakistan	1825	869	44	19.75	2	–
TOTAL	14199	6409	307	20.87	19	3

Abdul Qadir

First-class

	Balls	Runs	Wickets	Average	5w/inns	10w/match
			831	22.55.	66	18

Test cricket

	Balls	Runs	Wickets	Average	5w/inns	10w/match
v. Australia	3402	1613	45	35.86	3	1
v. England	5593	2049	82	24.98	8	4
v. India	1905	1045	21	49.76	–	–
v. New Zealand	1119	519	14	37.07	1	–
v. Sri Lanka	1007	453	14	32.35	1	–
v. West Indies	2208	1123	40	28.07	1	–
TOTAL	15234	6802	216	31.49	14	5

C. E. B. Rice

First-class

	Balls	Runs	Wickets	Average	5w/inns	10w/match
			882	22.18	21	1

Test cricket – nil

R. J. Shastri

First-class

	Balls	Runs	Wickets	Average	5w/inns	10w/match
			371	31.92	14	3

Test cricket

	Balls	Runs	Wickets	Average	5w/inns	10w/match
v. Australia	2158	769	21	36.61	–	–
v. England	3681	1288	28	46.00	–	–
v. New Zealand	1233	414	20	20.70	1	–
v. Sri Lanka	999	384	11	37.63	–	–
v. Pakistan	2556	926	22	42.09	1	–
v. West Indies	2775	1267	30	42.23	–	–
TOTAL	13402	5048	132	38.24	2	–

J. R. Thomson

First-class

	Balls	Runs	Wickets	Average	5w/inns	10w/match
			675	26.46	28	3

Test cricket

	Balls	Runs	Wickets	Average	5w/inns	10w/match
v. England	4951	2418	100	24.18	5	–
v. India	1167	516	22	23.45	–	–
v. New Zealand	534	192	6	32.00	–	–
v. Pakistan	1109	658	10	65.80	–	–
v. West Indies	2774	1818	62	29.32	3	–
TOTAL	10535	5602	200	28.01	8	–

D. L. Underwood

First-class

	Balls	Runs	Wickets	Average	5w/inns	10w/match
			2465	20.28	153	47

Test cricket

	Balls	Runs	Wickets	Average	5w/inns	10w/match
v. Australia	8000	2770	105	26.38	4	2
v. India	4995	1699	62	27.40	1	–
v. New Zealand	2118	586	48	12.20	6	3
v. Pakistan	2537	868	36	24.11	4	1
v. Sri Lanka	335	95	8	11.87	1	–
v. West Indies	3877	1656	38	43.57	1	–
TOTAL	21862	7674	297	25.83	17	6

R. G. D. Willis

First-class

	Balls	Runs	Wickets	Average	5w/inns	10w/match
			899	24.99	34	2

Test cricket

	Balls	Runs	Wickets	Average	5w/inns	10w/match
v. Australia	7294	3346	126	26.14	7	–
v. India	2941	1441	62	23.24	3	–
v. New Zealand	3018	1132	60	18.87	3	–
v. Pakistan	1772	820	34	24.12	1	–
v. Sri Lanka	168	70	3	23.33	–	–
v. West Indies	2164	1381	38	36.34	2	–
TOTAL	17357	8190	325	25.20	16	–